Energy Psychology Interactive
Self-Help Guide

Energy Psychology Interactive
Self-Help Guide

David Feinstein, Ph.D.

In consultation with Fred P. Gallo, Ph.D.,
Donna Eden, and the
Energy Psychology Interactive Advisory Board

Foreword by Candace Pert, Ph.D.

Keyed to the
Energy Psychology Interactive Book/CD Program
for Health Care Professionals

INNERSOURCE
Ashland, Oregon

INNERSOURCE, 777 East Main Street, Ashland, OR 975205
541-482-1800
www.innersource.net

Cover design by Tracy Baldwin

Library of Congress Control Nummber 2002114993

Catalog Information:
  Feinstein, David
    Energy Psychology Interactive Self-Help Guide
    First edition, paperback
      ISBN 0-9725207-6-7 (Pbk)
        1. Energy Psychology–Tutorial and Reference
        2. Self-Management–Psychology
        3. Healing–Psychological
        I. Title   2003
        616.89'1–DC 21

Printed in Canada

Dedicated to Jean Houston, a giant in our midst.

To learn more about the full *Energy Psychology Interactive* program for health care professionals, visit

www.EnergyPsychologyInteractive.com

Energy Psychology Interactive Advisory Board

Contents

Foreword[1]

OUR ABILITY TO HELP PEOPLE overcome self-defeating emotional patterns, achieve higher levels of psychological well-being, and open their spiritual sensibilities is accelerating at an extraordinary pace. This program introduces you to a powerful development within this unfolding story.

The biochemical underpinnings of awareness—of sensations such as pleasure and pain, drives such as hunger and thirst, emotions such as anger and joy, and "higher" states such as awe and spiritual inspiration—have been identified. "Informational substances" such as hormones, peptides, and neurotransmitters find their way—in one of nature's most stunning designs—to receptor molecules that are on the surface of every cell in the body.

These "molecules of emotion" shape mood and thought. Significantly, it is a two-way process. Emotions and thoughts initiate a series of cascading chemical events—including the formation of new neurons!—that are the basis of other emotions and thoughts. Some studies suggest, in fact, that meditation may be as effective as medication in alleviating anxiety and depression.

Energy Psychology Interactive is a synthesis of practices designed to deliberately shift the molecules of emotion. These practices have four distinct advantages over psychiatric medications. They are non-invasive, highly spe-

---

[1] Adapted for this Client Handbook from the Foreword to the *Energy Psychology Interactive* program for professionals.

cific, have no side effects, and they are free. Energy interventions are rooted in an emerging paradigm that is still just outside the embrace of Western science, though it has long been central to the worldview of Eastern medicine and spiritual disciplines.

These practices focus on the body's "energy system." The program you are about to begin teaches you how to influence these energies to shift patterns of emotion, thought, and behavior that are blatantly dysfunctional, or simply limiting.

Energy Psychology Interactive is an early formulation of a new field. It brings unfamiliar methods into the therapeutic arena, using tapping as much as talk, aiming for energy integration as much as insight. The procedures, as you will see, can look quite strange. The range of appropriate clinical and other applications is still being debated, but my personal impression, based on my own experience, is that it is enormous.

Energy Psychology Interactive brings these new methods to the therapist and, with this handbook, to anyone who wishes to apply them. David Feinstein was conducting research on psychotherapeutic innovations at the Department of Psychiatry of the Johns Hopkins University Medical School in the 1970s, the same time I was there doing my early work on the opiate receptor. Thirty years later his focus has turned to the intersection of psychotherapy and energy medicine. While he has practiced as a clinical psychologist during the intervening decades and in fact pioneered a powerful system for helping people transform their guiding myths, he has also accumulated some unusual credentials for a psychologist, not the least of which is that he is married to one of the world's most renowned energy healers, Donna Eden.

With *Energy Psychology Interactive*, Dr. Feinstein has culled through the wide range of practices being used by at least 5,000 psychotherapists whose work explicitly focuses on the body's energy systems. In consultation with Dr. Fred Gallo, author of several of the pioneering professional books on energy psychology, and Donna Eden, who provided the perspective of energy medicine, he identified the procedures that seemed the most promising, and he organized them into a systematic approach for introducing the field's basic methods to clinicians who are new to energy psychology. He then submitted this formulation to an advisory board of 24 of the field's leading thinkers and acknowledged innovators with the question, "Does this program cover the essential methods that clinicians who are new to energy psychology would need to learn in order to incorporate its methods into their practices?"

Because the field, new as it is, already has many factions, the critiques of the 24 people who form the advisory board led to literally hundreds of changes in the program, large and small, until the presentation represented a consensus of techniques and explanations. Based on this meticulous process, *Energy Psychology Interactive* is the most potent introduction available to clinicians who wish to incorporate this highly significant set of innovations into their practices. That state-of-the-art synthesis is reflected in this handbook.

Energy psychology has rapidly become one of the hottest areas of what I call "New Paradigm Medicine." Research is accumulating which suggests that healing the emotions is not only a gateway to a happier and more fulfilling life, it is a gateway to healing the body of virtually any physical illness. Energy psychology is a leading-edge therapy and *Energy Psychology Interactive* is a leading-edge way to learn it.

—**Candace Pert, Ph.D.**
Research Professor
Georgetown University School of Medicine

Introduction

I am teaching a six-day residential workshop in South Africa. Many of the participants are leaders in their communities who have come to learn about the unconscious beliefs and motivations that shape a person's life. The first evening, one of the participants tells the group that she is terrified of snakes and is afraid to walk through a grassy area from the meeting room to her cabin, about 100 feet away. Several participants offer to escort her. Sensing that she could rapidly be helped with this phobia, I arrange—with her tense but trusting permission—for a guide at the game reserve where the workshop is being held to bring a snake into the class at 10 a.m. the next morning.

I set up the chairs so the snake and the handler are 20 feet away from her, but within her range of vision. I ask her what it is like to have a snake in the room. She says, "I am okay as long as I don't look at it, but I have to tell you, I left my body two minutes ago." Within less than half an hour, using methods that you will learn with this handbook, she is able to imagine being close to a snake without feeling fear. I ask her if she is ready to walk over to the snake that is across the room. As she approaches the snake, she appears confident. The confidence has soon grown into enthusiasm as she begins to comment on the snake's beauty. She asks the handler if she can touch it. Haltingly but triumphantly, she does. She reports that she is fully present in her body. Her lifelong fear had evaporated, and on follow-up, has not returned.

The class is eager to learn the methods they have just seen demonstrated, and I teach them the same basic protocol presented in Part I of this guide. One of the women is borderline diabetic but is so phobic of needles that she has for years been putting off tests that are really a medical necessity. She asks for help with this. I invite someone from the group to work with her. It turns out that her roommate is the woman who had the fear of snakes, and she volunteers. The fear of needles is gone within a 45-minute session the two of them conduct outside the class. I learn later that the woman with the fear of needles made an appointment for lab tests the day the workshop ended and was calm and at ease as her blood was drawn. The methods that were used, which can be applied to a range of difficulties and goals, from reducing fear or jealousy to increasing confidence or assertiveness, originate from the field of energy psychology.

Energy psychology (used interchangeably with *energy-based psychotherapy* or simply *energy therapy*) is a powerful therapeutic approach that is utilized by an increasing number of therapists. It is a treatment method that can also be self-administered to help bring about positive personal changes.

This handbook was originally written as a back-home resource for people receiving the services of a health professional who is using energy-based methods. Designed to support the partnership between client and therapist, it is also proving a friendly and resourceful introduction to anyone interested in energy psychology.

How Emotional Problems Get Coded in Your Biochemistry

If you were to watch a PET scan (or any of a number of other modern imaging devices) of your brain while you are experiencing significant stress, anxiety, or trauma, you would see specific areas (particularly in the limbic system, which governs emotions, and the frontal cortex, which further interprets their meanings) receiving arousal signals that make the screen light up like a Christmas tree. Many emotional problems are brought about when memories, thoughts, or images cause the amygdala (a part of the limbic system) to evoke fear, aggression, or hyper-arousal, even though no trauma or threat is present.

If something you see or hear is unconsciously associated to a painful or traumatic situation from your past—even though there is no current danger—the same arousal signals that you experienced in the past situation can be triggered in your brain. The emotional response can be overwhelming, or it might be more subtle. You simply might not be able to think as clearly or you might experience distracting feelings that you do not understand. Though people often are not aware of it, this basic sequence is at the root of many dysfunctional patterns of emotion and behavior.

How Energy Psychology Helps

While energy psychology treatments have many dimensions, the core is this: Bring the psychological problem to mind and stimulate the energy points that counteract the brain's threat response. This rapidly retrains your nervous system to meet the psychological problem without slipping into painful, outdated, or limiting emotions, habits, or thought patterns.

Be forewarned that the procedures you are about to learn will look strange and you may be puzzled as to how they could possibly make a difference. Scientific research demonstrating their effectiveness is only now being conducted, but research in related areas is established. Anesthesia through acupuncture, for instance, is now used throughout the world and has been widely documented in procedures from appendectomies to brain surgery.

While this is challenging for many Westerners to assimilate into their world-views, it is a relatively small step from there to understanding how stimulating acupuncture points could relieve anxiety and other emotional problems.

The same principles can be applied not only to overcoming emotional *problems* but also for other types of self-improvement. Whatever your psychological goal—whether it is to overcome anxiety or increase your poise in public—imagining yourself in the situation while using energy techniques that optimize your brain's response is a powerful and effective aid.

Overview

This handbook will provide you with tools for conditioning your body's energies to overcome emotional problems, achieve psychological goals, and maximize inner well-being. The book is divided into three sections:

I. Addressing Specific Problems and Goals

Whatever the concerns you are addressing, your progress can be supported by insuring that your body's energies are in alignment with your goals for personal change. This constitutes the major section of the handbook. It teaches you procedures that are similar to what an energy-oriented therapist might use with you in the office, and it includes additional tools you might be shown for bolstering your progress at home.

II. Optimizing Your Energies

When the electromagnetic and other energies that animate your body are in an optimal harmony and flow, you feel healthy, alive, and full of vitality. While many factors determine the state of your energies, a number of exercises can enhance them for improved psychological functioning as well as overall health. A five-minute daily routine for optimizing your energies is presented in the second section of the handbook.

III. Uplifting Your Mood

One of the body's energy systems is directly involved with a person's degree of joy. This section shows you ways to stimulate and enliven these energies, called the "radiant circuits." The handbook closes with a list of useful website links and other resources.

What This Book Can Do and What It Can't Do

This book was originally written as a resource for psychotherapists to give to their clients for supporting and reinforcing the procedures being used in the office. Meanwhile, as substantial anecdotal evidence that the methods can be responsibly and effectively applied without the aid of a psychotherapist was accumulating (see, for instance, www.emofree.com, www.eft-innovations.com, www.instantemotionalhealing.com, and www.unstressforsuccess.com), the *Energy Psychology Interactive* Advisory Board elected to make it available to the general public.

The procedures can help you with many day-to-day psychological and emotional challenges, but you also need to be aware of some significant limitations. This book is not designed to work with *psychological illness* without the involvement of a qualified mental health professional. It is not designed as an independent "self-help" resource for the treatment of such conditions as major depression, severe anxiety, personality disorders, bipolar disorders, dissociative disorders, the aftermath of severe trauma or an assault to the body, substance abuse, or psychotic disorders. Please enlist the help of a qualified psychotherapist if you suffer from any of these conditions. Competent help is available to you. The techniques presented in this book may supplement the procedures used by a psychotherapist when serious psychological problems are present, but they do not substitute for them.

They may, however, be an effective resource in helping you negotiate the ups and downs of daily life and in reaching goals that have eluded you. The methods may be used to help you shift self-defeating patterns of thought or behavior. They may assist you in countering emotions that you consider intrusive or irrational, such as inappropriate anger, grief, guilt, jealousy, fear, attachment, self-judgment, worry, sadness, or shame. They may set you on a journey where you play the keyboard of your feelings more skillfully, regularly cultivating your emotional intelligence and inner harmony. They may lead you to various kinds of Internet, peer-help, and professional support, as appropriate, all available via the links at the end of this book. They are offered with the clear intention, shared by the leaders and innovators within the field of energy psychology who constitute the program's Advisory Board, that they will provide you with potent tools for navigating your way through life's challenges into a brighter and more productive day.

SECTION 1[1]

Energy Methods to Address Specific Problems and Goals

[1] Many elements from this section were written with generous consultation from Gary Craig and are based upon his Emotional Freedom Techniques (EFT). EFT is a revised formulation of Roger Callahan's Thought Field Therapy (TFT) that is particularly well-suited for self-help applications.

Section I: Energy Methods to Address Specific Problems and Goals

Overview

The Basic Concepts

Energy psychology is based on clinical findings showing that stimulating certain energy points on the skin alters psychological states.[2] Stimulating these points, while at the same time mentally holding images and thoughts related to a problem or goal, leads to shifts in neurochemistry, emotions, thoughts, and behavior.

Many psychological problems and goals lend themselves to energy-based interventions. Emotional and physical reactions, habits of thought, or patterns of behavior that get in your way can all be altered using the techniques of energy psychology. While many conditions should only be treated under the care of a qualified health professional, many therapists encourage their clients to use techniques such as those offered in this handbook to work independently with a variety of day-to-day problems, including:

- *Emotional reactions*, such as: "Every time I see a large dog, I feel fear that traces back to having been bitten as a child."
- *Physical reactions*, such as: "When I think of confronting my boss, I get a headache."
- *Habits of thought*, such as: "I worry obsessively that my daughter will not start a family until it is too late for her to have children."

---

[2] More detailed discussion, along with supporting theory and research, can be found in the *Energy Psychology Interactive* CD Program and companion book for health professionals.

- *Patterns of behavior,* such as: "I promise myself, over and over, that I will stop interrupting people when they are speaking with me, yet all of my relationships continue to suffer from this habit."

This section of the handbook presents a sequence of mechanical procedures you can use to shift the energetic and neurological underpinnings of these and similar problems. This often resolves or at least softens the problem, and at the same time can lead to a new understanding of it.

The Steps

1. Establishing an Energetic Receptiveness for Change

THE THREE THUMPS/THREE NAVEL TOUCH. Even before focusing on a psychological issue, a variety of techniques can be used to balance the energies in the nervous system and to optimize their flow. In addition to having generic health and psychological benefits, this will leave your body more receptive to subsequent energy interventions. While a more complete procedure is presented in Section II, a brief sequence of six simple techniques is taught here (all six can be done within 90 seconds). This sequence will, in many instances, improve the energetic balance of the nervous system and increase the effectiveness of the procedures you will be learning later. The six techniques are clustered into two simple sequences: the Three Thumps and the Three Navel Touch.

The Three Thumps

Certain points on your body, when tapped with your fingers, will affect your energy field in predictable ways, sending electrochemical impulses to targeted regions of your brain and releasing neurotransmitters.

Figure I.1

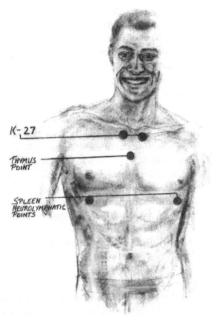

Drawing by Brooks Garten. Reproduced, with permission, from Donna Eden's *Energy Medicine*.

By tapping three specific areas, a sequence called the **Three Thumps**, you can activate a series of internal responses that will restore you when you are tired, increase your vitality, and keep your immune system stronger amidst stress. You can also tap these points any time you need a boost.

Do not be too concerned about finding the precise location of each point. If you use several fingers to tap in the vicinity shown on the drawing, you will hit the right spot. Tap hard enough that you hear the tap, but never so hard as to risk bruising yourself. Keep your attention on the tapping and your intention on improving the movement of energy throughout your body.

Thump	Approximate Time
K-27 Points	15–20 seconds
Thymus Gland	15–20 seconds
Spleen Points	15–20 seconds

K-27

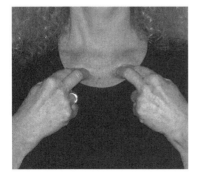

Thymus Gland

Spleen Points

The Three Navel Touch

Following the Three Thumps, breathe deeply as you perform:

1.   *The Navel/Skull Base Hold:* Find the soft area where the back of your neck merges with the base of your skull. Place your thumb and forefinger on this area with a bit of pressure. Place the middle finger of your other hand into your navel, push in, pull up. Hold for about 12 seconds.

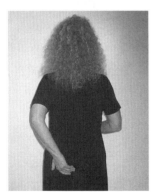

2.   *The Navel/Tailbone Massage:* Simultaneously hold or rub the tailbone and the navel for about 12 seconds.

3.   *The Navel/Third-Eye Hook-Up:* Place the middle finger of one hand on the third eye (between the eyebrows and above the bridge of the nose). Place the middle finger of the other hand in the navel. Gently push in and pull both fingers upwards for about 12 seconds.

This brief six-part sequence is worth memorizing and using whenever you are not functioning at your best, physically or mentally. It jump-starts your energy system, and it can help prepare you, energetically and neurologically, to make progress on problems that have been difficult to overcome.

2. Identifying and Rating a Problem That Is Suitable for Energy Interventions

IDENTIFYING A TARGET PROBLEM. The issue you focus on can involve a desired change in:

- an emotional response (e.g., "to overcome my fear of dogs"; "to feel confident when making a presentation")
- a physical reaction (e.g., "to stop these stress headaches in relationship to my boss"; "to stay calm and relaxed even when my spouse is treating me insensitively")
- a thought pattern (e.g., "to free myself of my obsession about my daughter's biological clock"; to "focus more on my son's strengths and achievements")
- a behavioral habit (e.g., "to stop interrupting people"; "to take more time to relax")

RATING THE TARGET PROBLEM. Once you have selected the issue you will focus on, give it a rating on a scale of 0 (no distress) to 10, based on the amount of distress you experience when you think about the problem. Use this rating as a gauge of your progress as you go through the procedures.

It is neither necessary nor desirable to re-live a past trauma in order to have a successful outcome using energy techniques. If the issue you are focusing on is a "hot" one emotionally, a variety of techniques can be used to keep the memory, situation, or feeling "at a distance." You could, for instance, give it a rating by "viewing" the memory or situation through a long tunnel. You could simply think about *what it would be like* to think about the issue. In his "tearless trauma" technique, when asking for a rating on the amount of distress caused by a traumatic memory, Gary Craig sometimes asks the client to simply "*guess* at what the emotional intensity would be [on the scale of 0 to 10] *if* you were to vividly imagine the incident."

If, on the other hand, you find yourself having difficulty getting your mind around the problem or accessing your feelings about it, you might take more time to attune inwardly while focusing and breathing deeply. You could vividly visualize circumstances that activate the problem, or slowly and deliberately replay in your imagination a situation in which you have in the past or might in the future experience the problem. Sometimes it is useful to make a mental "movie" of the situation.

Whether it works best for you to keep the problem at an emotional distance or make it more vivid, your task at this point is to rate the intensity of discomfort the problem or situation evokes in you *right now*, as you tune into it (as contrasted with what you *think* you would feel if you were in the situation again). Write down a number from 0 to 10 indicating the amount of distress it causes you to think about it, with 10 being an extreme amount and 0 being none at all.

3. Establishing a Psychological Receptiveness for Change

Whenever you decide to change a habit of thought, behavior, or emotion, the part of you that initially *established* that pattern may resist your efforts. Psychological and behavioral habits are often hard-won compromises, and they become embedded in your energy system as well as in your psyche. Your psyche and your energy system are designed to maintain strategies that have helped you survive. Whatever the shortcomings of the habit or pattern you want to change, you *have survived* under its watch, and parts of you that are outside your conscious awareness will not necessarily be receptive to your conscious efforts to change it. For example, you decide to be more supportive of your employees and find yourself being more critical than ever. You decide to set aside more time to relax and you find yourself taking on additional responsibilities.

Sometimes called a "psychological reversal" (because you wind up doing the reverse of what you intend), addressing unconscious conflict about a consciously desired outcome makes it much easier to reach your goal. Psychological reversals involve unconscious resistance to the consciously desired outcome as well as a resistance in the body's energy system. Remember the toy puzzle in which you stick a finger into each end of a straw tube and the harder you try to pull your fingers out, the more firmly they become embedded? That is how a psychological reversal feels: your efforts produce the opposite of the result you intend. All effective therapies address psychological reversals in one way or another. Until these are resolved, no other therapeutic intervention is likely to have a deep or lasting effect. Energy psychology focuses directly on the energetic as well as psychological roots of these reversals, resulting in some surprisingly simple ways to deal with this potential obstacle to taking greater charge of your life.

The Set-up Affirmation

While the psychological reversal is worthy of in-depth consideration,[3] you will learn here a simple technique that can resolve many psychological reversals, preparing the way psychologically and energetically for you to proceed toward your goal. This technique is referred to as the "set-up affirmation."[4] The two parts to the set-up affirmation are an *affirmation* and an *energy intervention* that involves rubbing a specific point on the body. The affirmation uses the following format:

---

[3] See Chapter 4 of the *Energy Psychology Interactive* book for health care professionals.

[4] The basic terms and procedure taught in EFT (Gary Craig's Emotional Freedom Techniques) are presented here.

> *Even though I have this* _____ *, I deeply love
> and accept myself.*

The blank is filled in with a brief description of the problem being addressed. For example:

- *Even though I have this fear of dogs, I deeply love and accept myself.*
- *Even though I get a headache when I think of confronting my boss, I deeply love and accept myself.*
- *Even though I have this obsession about my daughter's biological clock, I deeply love and accept myself.*
- *Even though I have this impulse to interrupt people, I deeply love and accept myself.*

Any psychological or behavioral problem or goal, from a craving for chocolate to difficulties with your tennis serve, can be translated into this format.

While the phrase "I deeply love and accept myself" might seem like an overly simple and pat self-affirmation, it actually penetrates to the heart of the psychological reversal. When you target something about yourself for change, the mechanisms for self-judgment and self-negation become engaged. This traces back to the way all parents and all cultures shape a child's thoughts, attitudes, and behavior. You have the idea "I want to exercise more regularly" and your self-esteem is held ransom when you do not carry out the desired behavior (or bring about a desired internal change). But the more you mobilize to force the change to happen, the more vehemently the parts of your psyche and energy system that are designed to maintan what has been established mobilize to resist the change.

A deep suggestion that fosters self-acceptance despite the unwanted pattern, made with focus and intent, tends to circumvent the entire sequence, relaxing both the self-negating mechanism and the resistance to your conscious intention. "I deeply love and accept myself" is usually effective. Other strong, positive, affirming statements may be a better fit, such as, "my intentions are pure."

The affirmation is best stated out loud, with feeling and emphasis. It does not matter whether or not you believe it to be a true statement, it is a self-suggestion that becomes more true in the process of saying it and stimulating specific energy points. Various alternative wordings are possible within the general format of acknowledging the problem and creating an affirmation of self-acceptance despite the existence of the problem. The format shown in the examples is easy to memorize and has been used widely with good reports.

Other formats emphasize choice and opportunity rather than self-acceptance,[5] such as, "Even though I have neglected my body, I choose to know that I deserve to have time for regular, enjoyable exercise," or, "Even though I still focus on my son's shortcomings, I choose to know that I deeply love and accept him." The strategy is to stimulate energy points that help pair a negative self-evaluation with a positive cognition or recognition of an opportunity. In essence, this programs the negative thought to become a trigger for a positive choice.

This method can be used even in situations that are bleak or overwhelming. A depressed client in his first psychotherapy session developed the affirmation, "Even though my life feels hopeless, I choose to find unexpected help in this therapy." Writing to her colleagues the day after 9-11 on how to assist people in dealing with the psychological aftermath of the attack, psychologist Patricia Carrington suggested using the Choices Method with phrasings such as "Even though I am stunned and bewildered by this terrible happening, I choose to learn something absolutely essential for my own life

---

[5] Developed as the Choices Method by psychologist Patricia Carrington, Ph.D., you can learn more about this approach at www.eft-innovations.com/Articles/collection.htm.

from this event," or "Even though . . . , I choose to be a still point amidst all the chaos," or "I choose to have this dreadful event open my heart," or "I choose to sense the Divine intent for a greater good in all this."

The Energy Intervention

An *energy intervention* is performed simultaneously with stating the set-up affirmation. The body's energy system can be affected by rubbing, tapping, stretching, holding, or tracing specific points or areas on the surface of the skin. The effectiveness of the set-up affirmation can be increased substantially by rubbing either or both of two points, called the "sore spots." Located in the upper left and right portions of the chest, you can find these spots by pressing in on various points until you find one or more that are sore. This is the area you will rub while stating the affirmation three times. You might want to rub an area on each side simultaneously.

Sore Spots

Karate Chop

The sore spots are lymphatic points where toxins tend to accumulate, thus blocking the flow of the body's energies. The soreness is usually felt because accumulations of toxins are broken apart when you rub the points, disbursing the toxins for elimination and opening a flow of energy to the heart, chest cavity, and entire body.

Rubbing a sore spot should not cause more than a little discomfort. If it does, apply less pressure. Also, if you have had an injury or operation in that area of the chest or if there is any other reason that you should not be massaging that specific area, switch to the other side. If there is a medical concern about massaging the chest sore spots, or if you cannot find a spot that is sore, an alternative energy intervention is to tap the "karate chop" points on the sides of your hands. A second alternative is to state the affirmation while doing the Navel/Third-Eye Hook-Up (see p. 14).

In summary, to enhance your psychological receptiveness for the desired change, repeat three times an affirmation in the form of "Even though [describe problem], I deeply love and accept myself." Simultaneously, rub the chest sore spots, tap the karate chop points, or do the Navel/Third-Eye Hook-Up.

4. Initial Round of Energy Interventions Focusing on the Problem

The initial round of energy interventions has three parts:

A. The tapping sequence
B. The bridging sequence
C. The tapping sequence (repeated)

A. The Tapping Sequence

The tapping sequence is concerned with the flow of energy through the body's *meridians*, or energy pathways. There are 14 major meridians and each is associated with points on the surface of the skin that, when tapped or otherwise stimulated, move the energy through the entire meridian system. Clinical reports suggest that working with only a subset of these points is usually necessary because the meridians are interconnected and stimulating one meridian can affect others. Various subsets have been used. The protocol you will learn here teaches you eight of the points used in Emotional Freedom Techniques and Thought Field Therapy:

Figure I.2
EFT EIGHT-POINT TREATMENT CHART

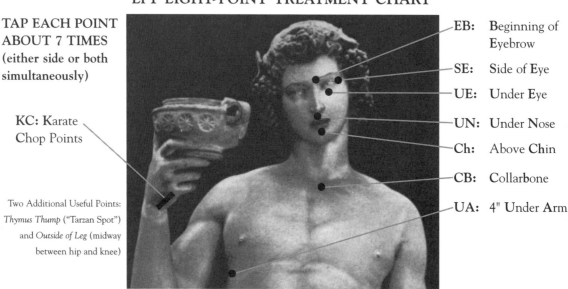

TAP EACH POINT ABOUT 7 TIMES (either side or both simultaneously)

KC: Karate Chop Points

Two Additional Useful Points: *Thymus Thump* ("Tarzan Spot") and *Outside of Leg* (midway between hip and knee)

EB:	Beginning of Eyebrow
SE:	Side of Eye
UE:	Under Eye
UN:	Under Nose
Ch:	Above Chin
CB:	Collarbone
UA:	4" Under Arm

Bacchus by Michelangelo (detail)

1. EB (for "Beginning of the Eyebrow") is at the beginning of the eyebrow, just above and to one side of the nose.

2. SE (for "Side of the Eye") is on the bone bordering the outside corner of the eye.

3. UE (for "Under the Eye") is on the bone under either eye, about one inch below the pupil.

4. UN (for "Under the Nose") is on the small area between the bottom of the nose and the top of the upper lip.

5. Ch (for "Chin") is midway between the point of the chin and the bottom of the lower lip (while not exactly on the point of the chin, the term "chin point" is descriptive enough for people to understand and remember easily).

6. CB (for "Collarbone") is the junction where the sternum (breastbone), collarbone, and the first rib meet (you learned this point earlier as "K-27").

7. UA (for "Under the Arm") is about four inches below the armpit, about even with the nipple (for men) or in the middle of the bra strap for women.

8. KC (for "Karate Chop" points) are in the middle of the fleshy part on the outside of either hand, between the top of the wrist bone and the base of the baby finger (the part of your hand you would use to deliver a karate chop).

The tapping points proceed down the body. Each is below the one before it. This makes them easy to memorize. A few trips through the sequence, Gary Craig tells his students, and it should be yours forever.

HOW TO TAP. Tapping can be done with either hand, or both hands simultaneously or in sequence. You can tap with the fingertips of your index finger and middle finger, or make a "3-finger notch" by including your thumb. Tap solidly but never so hard as to hurt or risk bruising yourself.

Tap about seven times on each of the tapping points or, alternatively, for the length of a deep inhalation and exhalation. You will be repeating a "reminder phrase" (see below) while you are tapping, so you will not be counting, and it does not matter if you tap a few more or a few less than seven.

Most of the tapping points exist on both sides of the body. It does not matter which side you use, and there might be some benefits to tapping both sides simultaneously. It might also be beneficial to alternate between the sides, tapping the left point once, then the right, then the left, etc. For the last area—the karate chop points—tap the entire length of the fleshy part of the side of the hand with all four fingers of the other hand.

Some people prefer other means than tapping for stimulating the energy points. One method is to massage the points. In another, called Touch and

Breathe,[6] you touch the point lightly with one or two fingers and take a complete breath (one easy inhalation and one easy exhalation, at your own pace, usually through the nose). You can then move on to the next point.

THE REMINDER PHRASE. Specific memories, thoughts, or circumstances cause disruptions in the energy system and elicit related negative emotions. If the problem from which you want relief is a fear of heights, that fear is not present while you are thinking about what to have for lunch. For an energy treatment to have an effect on your target problem, that problem must be "activated" within your energy system.

A *problem state* can be activated by simply thinking about it. Bringing the problem to mind disrupts the meridian energies, which can then be re-established by applying the treatment. Balancing the meridian energy while thinking about the problem retrains the body to be able to hold the thought, or be in the circumstance, without creating the energy disruption that then impacts thoughts, feelings, and behavior. *When the energy is not disturbed, the negative emotion associated with that energy disturbance is not triggered.*

You may, however, find it a bit difficult to consciously think about the problem while you are doing the other treatment procedures. By continually repeating a *reminder phrase* while performing the procedures, you keep yourself attuned to the situation that has been triggering the disruption in your energy system. This has been compared to keeping a radio dialed to the right station.

The reminder phrase is a word or short phrase describing the problem. You repeat it out loud each time you tap one of the points in the tapping sequence. This activates the psychological, neurological, and energetic components of your problem. The reminder phrase is often identical or very close to the phrase used in the set-up affirmation. For example, if you were focusing on a memory in which you were humiliated as a child while performing in front of an audience, the set-up affirmation might be:

---

[6] Developed by psychologist John Diepold, Ph.D.

> *Even though I feel humiliated by [what happened at the eighth-grade play], I deeply love and accept myself.*

Within this affirmation, the words "humiliated by what happened at the eighth-grade play" can be used as the reminder phrase. Abbreviated versions of the statement, such as "humiliated at the play," or simply "humiliated," will also suffice as long as their full meaning is clear to you. The reminder phrase might be as simple as (referencing back to the earlier examples):

- fear of large dogs (or simply "fear" or "large dogs")
- headaches about confronting my boss (or simply "headaches" or "confronting my boss")
- obsession about Mary's biological clock (or simply "obsession" or "biological clock")
- impulse to interrupt people (or simply "impulse" or "interrupting people")

The following additional reminder phrases suggest the range of possible areas for energy interventions: craving for sweets, my role in the accident, lower-back pain, anger toward my sister, appearing in court, ambivalence about my boyfriend, fired, fear of elevators, depression, stock losses, terrorist attack, divorce. The more specific the reminder phrase, or at least the more specific the problem it stands for is in your mind, the more effective the phrase will be.

B. The Bridging Sequence

Activities that stimulate certain areas of the brain appear to increase the effectiveness of subsequent energy interventions. Specific parts of the brain are stimulated when the eyes are moved, and various therapies, such as Eye

Movement Desensitization and Reprocessing (EMDR, www.emdr.com) utilize this principle. The most widely used eye movement technique within energy psychology is Roger Callahan's Nine Gamut Procedure. It is introduced here along with the comment that it is one of the more strange-looking procedures in energy psychology, with the tapping, eye movements, humming, and counting all designed to stimulate specific parts of the brain. While not directly targeting the problem with a reminder phrase, the Nine Gamut Procedure bridges two tapping sequences that do.

In the Nine Gamut Procedure, one of the body's energy spots, the "gamut point," is continuously tapped while nine simple steps are carried out. The gamut point is on the back of either hand, 1/2 inch below the knuckles (toward the wrist), and in line with the midpoint between the little finger and the ring finger. While tapping the gamut point continuously, perform the following nine actions:

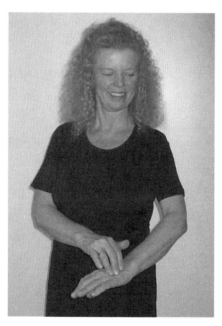

1. Close eyes.
2. Open eyes.
3. Move eyes to lower left.
4. Move eyes to lower right.
5. Rotate eyes clockwise 360 degrees (alternative: move in a figure-eight).
6. Rotate eyes counter-clockwise 360 degrees (alternative: reverse direction of the eight).
7. Hum a tune for a few seconds (e.g., "Happy Birthday," "Row, Row Your Boat," "Zipadee Doo Dah").
8. Count to five.
9. Hum again.

Other bridging procedures, such as a brisk walk around the room with an exaggerated arm motion (opposite arm moving with opposite leg), or walking in place, can also be used. Sometimes the Nine Gamut is ended as follows: "Bring your eyes down to the floor and then slowly bring them up to the ceiling, projecting your sight out into the distance as your eyes move up the arc."

C. *The Tapping Sequence Repeated*

EFT speaks of the treatment "sandwich," which involves:

1. Tapping sequence (with reminder phrase)
2. Nine Gamut procedure
3. Tapping sequence (with reminder phrase)

In the second tapping sequence, you repeat the first one exactly as you did it earlier. When you have completed the second sequence of tapping, you would again assess the intensity of the problem: Close your eyes, bring the original problem to mind, and give it a rating from 0 to 10 on the amount of distress it causes you *now*, as you think about it.

If you can get no trace whatsoever of your previous emotional intensity, the next step is to challenge the results (see below). If, on the other hand, you go down to, lets say, a 4, you would perform subsequent rounds until, ideally, 0 is reached (2 is often all that is required for the problem to essentially be resolved). Each round requires just over one minute.

5. Subsequent Rounds

Sometimes a problem is resolved after a single round of treatment. More often, only partial relief is obtained and additional rounds are necessary. Two simple adjustments need to be made for these subsequent rounds.

1. **Psychological Reversals.** A possible obstacle to success during the first round of treatment is the reemergence of *psychological reversals*, the internal conflicts the set-up affirmation was designed to resolve.

After treatment has begun and some progress has been made, the psychological reversal takes on a somewhat different quality. It is no longer preventing any change in the condition being treated, but it might be interfering with further progress. The wording of the set-up affirmation needs to reflect this. The set-up affirmation is a self-suggestion targeted to the unconscious mind, which tends to be very literal, so its wording should focus on the way the problem is still present. A slight adjustment—the addition of two words—accomplishes this. The adjusted format for the set-up affirmation is:

> *Even though I **still** have **some** of this _____,*
> *I deeply love and accept myself.*

The words "still" and "some" shift the emphasis of the affirmation toward a focus on the remainder of the problem. The adjustment is easy to make. The affirmations below reflect adjustments to the affirmations listed earlier:

- *Even though I **still** have **some** of this fear of dogs, I deeply love and accept myself.*
- *Even though I **still** get a headache when I think of confronting my boss, I deeply love and accept myself.*
- *Even though I **still** have **some** of this obsession about my daughter's biological clock, I deeply love and accept myself.*
- *Even though I **still** have **some** of this impulse to interrupt people, I deeply love and accept myself.*

2. The **Reminder Phrase** also needs a minor adjustment. Simply place the word "remaining" in front of the original reminder phrase. Here as examples are adjusted versions of the reminder phrases presented earlier:

- *remaining fear of large dogs* (or simply *"remaining fear"*)
- *remaining headaches about confronting my boss* (or simply *"remaining headaches"*)
- *remaining obsession about Mary's biological clock* (or simply *"remaining obsession"*)
- *remaining impulse to interrupt people* (or simply *"remaining impulse"*)

Following each round, do a new 0 to 10 assessment of the distress you now feel when you tune into the original problem. If the level of distress continues to decrease, do subsequent rounds until you reach 0 or until the distress stops decreasing.

Sometimes the rating will get down to a 2 or a 1 but will not reduce any further. This is not necessarily a bad outcome. For some problems, you might not be able to conceive of the rating going down to 0, and a 1 or a 2 is essentially a "cure" in your subjective world. In some circumstances, such as taking a test, a small measure of anxiety increases your ability to function. So while 0 might be thought of as the ideal, it is not always realistic or necessary.

If you are still able to activate disturbing feelings in relationship to the problem, continue working with the procedures described above until you are unable to feel distress in relationship to the image or incident, or unable to lower the degree of distress you do feel. If after five rounds the rating is still not down to 0 or near 0, you may need to shift your focus or wording, or you may have identified a problem where you need outside assistance. There are many possible reasons that improvement becomes stalled. A small proportion of people do not respond to tapping the standard energy points (if you suspect you are one of them, try massaging the points or simply touching each point while breathing deeply). The problem might need to be formulated with more specific or altogether different wording. Internal conflict about resolving the problem might need greater exploration. *Aspects* of the problem that are not being addressed might need to be identified and treated. The aspects of a problem are discussed below. By understanding and working with them, you can laser focus the techniques in a way that will further reduce the distress you experience when the problem is activated.

Once you do get the subjective distress rating down to 0 or near 0, the next step is to "challenge" it. Try to recall or visualize the situation in a manner that evokes the earlier sense of distress. If the disturbed energy pattern has been corrected—that is, if the earlier memory, thought, or situation is now paired to a stable response in your energy system—you will not be able to activate your earlier feelings. The speed with which this can often be accomplished is among the most striking benefits of energy psychology. A difficult situation will still be recognized for its inherent dangers, injuries, or injustices, but the stress response in your central nervous system that had been paired with that situation will no longer be triggered.

If you are unable to reproduce any trace of the initial emotional response, the probability is strong that the issue has been deactivated and you can expect to meet provocative circumstances with a reasonable degree of confidence. The subsequent discussion on translating inner change to daily life will further support your ability to bring these gains into challenging situations.

Addressing Different Aspects of the Problem

The most common reason the distress rating would not have gone down to 0 or close to 0 if you followed the instructions precisely is that another aspect of the problem is involved that was not focused upon in the energy intervention. While many psychological issues are just what they appear to be and have no hidden aspects, complex psychological problems can have numerous aspects, and an apparently successful treatment is less likely to prove durable unless each aspect is addressed. A recent trauma or loss, for example, often unearths a network of earlier traumas or losses. Think of peeling the layers of an onion.

Suppose that at some point in your childhood you were bitten by a dog. This memory has long been forgotten and is apparently resolved. But then you hear of a neighbor receiving a serious dog bite, and you develop a fear of dogs rated at a 9, which generally involves a level of physiological arousal that suggests more is at play than just having heard a single incident reported. The tapping methods might reduce this fear a bit, but it is not likely they will be very effective until the childhood incident has been addressed. Actually, chances are that in doing the self-treatment around the current fear, memories of having been bitten as a child, will emerge. The focus can then easily be shifted to them. Having been bitten as a child is an *aspect* of "fear of dogs," and it needs attention before the fear of dogs can be successfully addressed.

The aspects might include earlier experiences that are involved in the current problem, but they might also slice in from different angles. An aspect can be a particular feeling or sensory experience that is involved with the problem. Perhaps the feeling of having been humiliated was an aspect of the memory that requires attention. Perhaps you blamed yourself for being bitten. Seeing your own blood might be an aspect of the problem. A vivid memory of how the dog smelled might linger as an aspect of the problem, or the helplessness of seeing the dog baring his teeth, about to attack. This might then tie into other memories of feeling helpless that must have their emotional charge neutralized before the original problem can be fully resolved. Most complex psychological goals and problems have numerous aspects. Identifying the most relevant aspect to focus on is part of the art of energy psychology.

According to Gary Craig, many who use energy-based interventions would increase their effectiveness if they were more specific in their formulations about the issues they target. Rather than focus on a global condition, such as "anxiety," he recommends identifying specific experiences, often from childhood, that involve the condition, or current situations that trigger it, and neutralizing the emotional charge to them, one by one, until this eventually generalizes to all related situations.

6. Translating Inner Change to Daily Life

Once you have shifted your internal response to a memory, image, or situation so it is no longer problematic, the change will often carry into your daily life. Your energy system and your neurochemistry have been reprogrammed. You can do a number of things, however, to reinforce the change and to counter the force of provocative circumstances. The first, the "Auric Weave," is a simple way of stabilizing the energies in their new configuration. The second involves a kind of "rehearsal" in which you visualize yourself having an optimal response in a challenging situation, and you adjust your energies to support this vision.

THE AURIC WEAVE. The human biofield is an electromagnetic field, detectable using established measuring instruments, that comes several inches out from the skin and surrounds the entire body. This biofield is probably the basis of the concept of the *aura*. It is believed to be like an envelope that *contains* your own energies while protecting you from harmful energies in the environment and simultaneously *connecting* you with other energies. Energy healers report that the health of the biofield or aura reflects the health of the body, as well as its vulnerability to taking on diseases and other outside intrusions.

Because your hands carry an electromagnetic charge, you can use them to smooth, trace, and strengthen your biofield—this is almost like giving it a massage. The biofield seems to have the best response when "massaged" in figure-eight patterns. When your energies are in a positive state, you can use your hands to "weave your aura" so that it constitutes itself around this positive state. Hold the image that initially triggered the problem, with the distress level now at 0 or close enough to 0 that you would like to "lock it in," and you can energetically reinforce this internal state by weaving your aura as follows:

1. With your feet firmly planted, rub your hands together. Then bring your hands a few inches apart and notice if you feel an energy charge between them. Whether or not you can detect it, it is there, and you will be using it to magnetically weave the energies on the surface of your body in figure-eight patterns.
2. Take a deep breath as you hold your hands about six inches from your ears. Tune into the image or thought that no longer evokes a stress reaction.
3. Make small figure-eights at your ears and begin to increase the movement until your hands are making small and large figure-eight patterns all the way down your body, on the sides, front, and back. Use a free-flow rather than rigid structure, moving the energy to your own inner rhythm.
4. As you do so, imagine that you are weaving your energies into a seamless fabric. You may want to move to a favorite piece of music.

BRIDGING THE INNER CHANGE INTO YOUR BEHAVIOR. A series of steps[7] that are quite similar to what you have already learned can help anchor the positive internal changes in your daily life. Each step is followed by a description taken from the dog bite example.

---

[7] Patterned after the "Outcome Projection Procedure" developed by Fred P. Gallo, Ph.D.

1. Vividly visualize or otherwise imagine a situation that would induce the old response. *A man who has been neutralizing his fear of dogs imagines coming to a neighbor's house where a friendly but large dog is barking upon his approach.*

2. Visualize or imagine responding to or handling that situation in a manner you consider ideal. *The man imagines himself calmly putting his hand out for the dog to smell and speaking reassuringly to the dog.*

3. Rate, on a scale of 0 to 10, how believable this scene is to you. This time, the higher the number the more favorable the score. *This scene, while desirable, does not feel particularly believable to the man. He rates it at a 3.*

4. State a set-up affirmation around the issue while rubbing your chest sore spots or using one of the other energy interventions described on pages 21–22. The format for the set-up affirmation at this point focuses on the believability of the scene, such as: *Even though it is hard for me to believe that* [I could calmly put my hand out for the dog to sniff], *I deeply love and accept myself.*

5. Do a series of tapping/bridging/tapping sequences until the rating is at least up to 8. Keep active in your mind the vision or sense of handling the situation in a manner you consider ideal. Also give a name to this scene and use it as a reminder phrase while you are visualizing or sensing the scene. *After four rounds of tapping while seeing the scene and stating "comfortable with dogs," the believability of the scene where the man puts out his hand for the dog to smell has increased to 9.*

6. Whenever you are in or about to enter a situation that starts to evoke the old response, use the earlier set-up/tapping/bridging/tapping routine to further neutralize that response, and follow it with the above five steps. *The man arranges to visit a friend who has a large dog and uses the techniques to prepare for the visit and for whenever anxiety begins to arise.*

You might use a tapping routine focused on an emotional response you have just successfully transformed twice a day for a period of time, as well as whenever unwanted emotions connected to that problem arise. Applying the above procedure twice per day for several days will reinforce the gains. As with changing any habit, persistence will improve your results.

A SIMPLE PROCEDURE TO KEEP IN YOUR "BACK POCKET." A deceptively simple procedure can be used when you need a "quick fix" to calm an emotion or change an inner reaction that troubles you. It combines a self-affirmation with a simple tapping technique:[8]

1. Begin by rating the problem on the amount of distress you feel when you think about it, using the 0 to 10 scale you learned earlier.
2. Fold your arms, rest your fingers on your bicep muscles, and pat your right and left biceps alternately with your hands, about a second for each tap (the "butterfly hug").
3. Continuing the butterfly hug and tapping, state aloud an affirmation in the form you learned earlier, "*Even though I [have this problem], I deeply love and accept myself*" (or end with a different strong, positive, affirming statement).
4. Take a deep breath or two, hugging and supporting yourself.
5. Reassess the amount of distress that thinking about the problem causes you on the 0 to 10 scale.
6. Repeat until the rating has gone down as low as you can get it.

If you have been able to get the rating down to 2 or less, you can finish by repeating the procedure with a positive affirmation. Use steps 2, 3, and 4 as above, but this time the affirmation describes what you would consider an ideal response in a situation that might have triggered the troubling emotion, such as "I can speak in front of any audience with confidence and comfort, and the universe supports me in every way" (or "and God loves me" or another closing phrase that evokes a positive, assuring feeling).

---

[8] This procedure, suggested by psychiatrist Daniel J. Benor, M.D., blends methods used in EMDR (Eye Movement Desensitization and Reprocessing) and EFT (Emotional Freedom Techniques).

Energy interventions can be used for past, present, or future issues. Often the current problem traces to experiences from the past that carry an intrusive emotional charge and can be cleared using an energy intervention. For help in the present moment, being able to use an energy intervention in the midst of a challenging event is an enormously comforting and useful skill to carry with you. Visualizing yourself handling an upcoming situation in a manner you consider ideal, and optimizing your energies while holding that vision, projects the response into your future.

> Once you have studied the material presented in this section, the following overview can help you to quickly review the principles. Once you are familiar with the basic principles, the list on p. 67 can quickly guide you through the basic procedures. You may copy it for easy reference.

Addressing Specific Problems and Goals: A Step-by-Step Guide

1. Establishing an Energetic Receptiveness for Change

The Three Thumps: K-27/Thymus/Spleen (p. 13)
The Three Navel Touch: Touch navel and base of skull, then tailbone, then third eye (p. 14)

2. Identifying and Rating a Problem That Is Suitable for Energy Interventions

Identify an emotional response, physical reaction, thought pattern, or behavioral pattern you would like to change and rate it from 0 to 10 according to the amount of distress you feel when you bring it to mind (p. 15).

3. Establishing a Psychological Receptiveness for Change

State the set-up affirmation (p. 17) three times in the format of: *Even though I* [describe problem], *I deeply and completely accept myself.* Simultaneously rub chest sore spots, tap karate chop points, or hold navel and third eye (p. 20).

4. Initial Round of Energy Interventions Focusing on the Problem ("The Sandwich")

A. Tap the standard energy points (EB, SE, UE, UN, Ch, K-27, UA, karate chop, as in Figure I-2 on p. 22) approximately seven times each while stating the reminder phrase at each point.

B. Bridging sequence: close eyes, open eyes, move eyes down to right, down to left, circle eyes right, circle left, hum, count, hum (p. 26).

C. Tap each point, again approximately seven times each while stating the reminder phrase (p. 27).

5. Subsequent Rounds of "The Sandwich"

Add "still" and "some" to the set-up affirmation (p. 28); add "remaining" to the reminder phrase (p. 29). Repeat up to five times.

6. Translating Inner Change to Daily Life

Do the Auric Weave (p. 33). Visualize an ideal response and pair it with the tapping sequence (p. 34).

SECTION II

Optimizing Your Energies

ENERGY INTERVENTIONS for resolving psychological problems are more effective if the energies that support brain function are flowing and balanced. Even in the course of a normal day, the nervous system can lose its optimal organization and performance, like a circuit board that picks up static electricity. Sleep is among nature's most effective ways of restoring the nervous system. Exercise is another.

When stress or other factors prevent the energies in the nervous system from reconstituting, day after day, year after year, the habitual disturbance reduces a person's resilience, clarity of mind, and overall health. Energy healers have developed a range of techniques to restore an optimal flow to the energies that affect the nervous system. While this is another large topic,[1]

---

[1] See Chapter 3 of the *Energy Psychology Interactive* book for health care professionals.

this section provides a five-minute daily energy routine—a set of procedures that have been found to be quite effective for optimizing the body's energies and enhancing the functioning of the nervous system to promote clear thinking, ease of learning, and overall vitality.[2] They include:

1. The Three Thumps
2. The Cross Crawl (with or without the Homolateral Crossover)
3. The Wayne Cook Posture
4. The Crown Pull
5. The Spinal Flush
6. The Zip-Up/Hook-Up

The Three Thumps
Time: About one minute.

You learned the Three Thumps on page 13. In brief:

Thump	Approximate Time
K-27 Points	15–20 seconds
Thymus Gland	15–20 seconds
Spleen Points	15–20 seconds

---

[2] This routine is excerpted, with permission, from Chapter 3 of Donna Eden's *Energy Medicine* (New York: Penguin Putnam, 1999). The drawings are by Brooks Garten.

The Cross Crawl
Time: About one minute.

The Cross Crawl is as simple as marching in place:

Figure II.1

1. While standing, lift your right arm and left leg simultaneously.
2. As you let them down, raise your left arm and right leg. If you are unable to do this because, for instance, of a physical disability, simply lift your knees to the opposite elbows, or twist your upper torso so your arm passes over the midline of your body.
3. Repeat, this time exaggerating the lift of your leg and the swing of your arm across the midline to the opposite side of your body.
4. Continue in this exaggerated march for at least one minute, again, breathing deeply in through your nose and out through your mouth.

Exception: If your energies are entrenched in a "homolateral pattern," the Cross Crawl is less likely to be effective. It will feel like pushing upstream. If the Cross Crawl is making you tired rather than vitalized, the Homolateral

Crossover can bring your energies into a crossover pattern so the Cross Crawl can then be effective.

The Homolateral Crossover

1. Begin with the Three Thumps and a full-body stretch that "reaches for the stars."
2. March in place, lifting right arm with right leg and then left arm with left leg.
3. Breathe deeply throughout the entire routine.
4. After about 12 lifts of the arms and legs in this homolateral pattern, stop and change the pattern to a normal Cross Crawl (lifting opposite arms and legs) for about 12 lifts.
5. Repeat the pattern twice more.
6. Anchor it with an additional dozen Cross Crawls and the Three Thumps.

The Wayne Cook Posture
Time: About two minutes.

To begin the Wayne Cook Posture, sit in a chair with your spine straight:

1. Place your right foot over your left knee. Wrap your left hand around your right ankle and your right hand around the ball of your right foot.

2. Breathe in slowly through your nose, letting the breath lift your body as you breathe in. At the same time, pull your leg toward you, creating a stretch. As you exhale, breathe out of your mouth slowly, letting your body relax. Repeat this slow breathing and stretching four or five times.

3. Switch to the other foot. Place your left foot over your right knee. Wrap your right hand around your left ankle and your left hand around the ball of your left foot. Use the same breathing.

4. Uncross your legs and place your fingertips together, forming a pyramid. Bring your thumbs to rest on your third eye, just above the bridge of your nose. Breathe slowly in through your nose. Then breathe out through your mouth, allowing your thumbs to separate slowly across your forehead, pulling the skin.

5. Slowly bring your hands down in front of you. Surrender into your breathing.

The Crown Pull
Time: About 15 seconds.

While doing the Crown Pull, breathe deeply in through your nose and out through your mouth:

Figure II.2

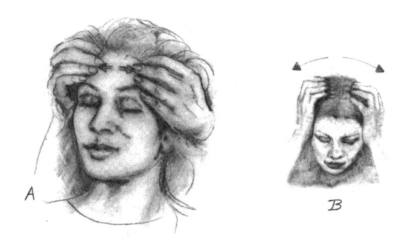

1. Place your thumbs at your temples on the side of your head. Curl your fingers and rest your fingertips just above the center of your eyebrows.
2. Slowly, and with some pressure, pull your fingers apart so that you stretch the skin just above your eyebrows.
3. Rest your fingertips at the center of your forehead and repeat the stretch.
4. Rest your fingertips at your hairline and repeat the stretch.
5. Continue this pattern, fingers curled and pushing in at each of these locations:
   a. Fingers at the top of your head, with your little fingers at the hairline. Push down with some pressure and pull your hands away from one another, as if pulling your head apart.

b. Fingers at the center of your head, again pushing down and pulling your hands away from one another.

c. Fingers over the curve at the back of your head, again using the same stretch.

d. Repeat each of these stretches one or more times.

The Spinal Flush
Time: About one minute.

THE SPINAL FLUSH WITH A PARTNER

If you wake up tired, doing the spinal flush will bring fresh energy to you; if you are sore in the evening, it will relax you. It is a particularly nice procedure to do with a friend.

1. Lie face down, or stand three or four feet from a wall and lean into it with your hands supporting you. This positions your body to remain stable while your partner applies pressure to your back.

2. Have your partner massage the points down both sides of your spine, using the thumbs or middle fingers and applying body weight to get strong pressure. Massage from the bottom of your neck all the way down to the bottom of your sacrum.

3. Have your partner go down the notches between your vertebrae and deeply massage each point. Staying on the point for at least five seconds, your partner moves the skin up and down or in a circular motion with strong pressure.

4. Upon reaching your sacrum, your partner can repeat the massage or can complete it by sweeping the energies down your body. From your shoulders, and with open hands, your partner sweeps all the way down your legs and off your feet, two or three times.

Do not worry about a point being missed. Each of your meridians will be covered by simply going between all of the notches. Rather than knowing which meridians are associated with which points, simply ask for special attention on any points that are sore.

THE SPINAL FLUSH WITHOUT A PARTNER

If you do not have a partner available to work the reflex points on your back, there are still many points on your back that you can reach and clear by reaching over your shoulders or around your waist and pushing into the notches yourself. Also, find any sore spots on the front of your body. Wherever you have tenderness, massage these points for several seconds. While the tenderness will not necessarily go away immediately, you are clearing the congestion. This self-massage, which focuses on neurolymphatic points, is valuable to do on a daily basis. It clears congestion that blocks the flow of vital energies. You will feel a difference.

The Zip-Up/Hook-Up
Time: 30 seconds.

To Zip Up:

1. Briskly tap the K-27 points to assure that your meridians are moving in a forward direction.
2. Place your hand at the bottom end of the central meridian, which is at your pubic bone.
3. Take a deep breath in as you simultaneously move your hand with deliberation straight up the center of your body to your lower lip.
4. Repeat three times.

The Navel/Third-Eye Hook-Up

As you learned earlier, place the middle finger of one hand over your third eye (between the eyebrows, above the bridge of the nose) and the middle finger of the other hand over the belly button. Gently press in, pull up, and hold for about 20 seconds.

SECTION III

Uplifting Your Mood

THE CAPACITY FOR JOY is wired into your body, carried along a network called the *radiant circuits*, whose energies are crucial for maintaining health as well as feeling good. When the *radiant energies* move, they bring strength and resilience, joy and vitality. These energies are a precious resource, and it is the body's design that they jump to wherever they are most needed. Beyond doing repair work, these are also primary energies in exhilaration, falling in love, orgasm, hope, gratitude, rapture, and spiritual ecstasy. Called the *strange flows, collector meridians,* or *extraordinary vessels* in traditional Chinese medicine, they are actually not exactly flows, meridians, or vessels. More like hyperlinks on the Web, they jump instantly to wherever they need to go, which is one reason the Chinese found them to be both strange and extraordinary. Through them all of the body's energy systems are linked and energetic deficiencies and excesses regulated. Because they are associated with the awakening of psychic abilities and the capacity to channel healing energies into the body, they sometimes were called *psychic channels*.

While the radiant circuits are a largely neglected topic, as they are only beginning to be scientifically investigated, they are a potentially invaluable area for anyone concerned with psychological well-being. The term *radiant* is used because people who "see" energy experience this force as carrying a radiant glow; the term *circuits* is used because one of the most important functions of this network is to create instant circuits that distribute energies throughout the body. The radiant circuits not only carry a radiant charge that connects all the energies and energy systems of the body, they are also attuned to and fed by the most vital energies of the environment, particularly the interpersonal environment. Just as they literally have a radiant appearance to people who are able to see energies, the radiant circuits bring a radiant, healing, uplifting quality to every system they touch.

A number of energy-based techniques for "turning up the volume" on your radiant energies can be self-applied, and that is the purpose of this section.[1] The radiant circuits, serving as inner wells of joy, support a vibrancy and a harmony throughout the entire body and energy system. If your radiant circuits are not flowing, you cannot feel joy. It is that simple. And if they are not doing their essential task of connecting and harmonizing among all your energy systems, you will be disjointed as you move through your life.

Seven Easy Turn-Ons

Working with the radiant circuits can itself set off waves of energy that feel good. At the same time, they connect the meridian lines, help the chakras spin, and engage all of the other energies. But they do not lend themselves easily to formulas. The only "formula" is to model yourself after the radiant

---

[1] For more depth and detail, see The Radiant Energies module on the CD that is included in the *Energy Psychology Interactive* program for professionals.

energy itself, which is to be absolutely spontaneous. Think of a surge of excitement, falling in love, becoming enchanted. The radiant circuits are literally and figuratively the polar opposite of "staying on track" (a special endowment of the meridians).

Many things you do naturally and spontaneously activate the radiant circuits. Joy begets joy. A natural, spontaneous smile sends joy all the way down to your core and up again. A deep smile is not an ornament or a mask. It engages your radiant energies. So does listening to music you love, being overtaken by beauty, reveling in nature, laughing uncontrollably, abandoning yourself in play, love, or dance; as does anything that moves out negative thoughts, painful emotions, or stagnant energies, including exercise, laughter, or energy techniques. But it is also the case that if you don't use it, you really do lose it. The radiant energies can become stagnant and unable to move easily to where they are needed. This is the plight of many of us today where work, computer screens, and passive entertainment have taken precedence over deeper pleasures. The more the radiant energies are exercised, the more available they are to you.

All of the exercises presented here work best if you enjoy them. Enjoyment stimulates the radiant energies. So as with the rest of life, your attitude is of consequence here. Seven simple ways to turn on the radiant energies are:

1. *Blow Out and Zip Up*. When you are feeling tight, depressed, or overwhelmed—as if you have become a collector of stress, anger, or disappointment—stand with your hands on your thighs, fingers spread, take a deep breath in, and then exhale. With your next deep inhalation, make fists and swing your arms up and around until they are high above your head. Then turn your hands so that your knuckles are facing

toward you. Bring your fisted hands down swiftly, opening them as you blow out the accumulated stress with force. Repeat as often as feels good. On the last repetition, move your arms down slowly and deliberately on the exhale. Next, with a slow, deep in-breath, open your hands, move them in front of your thighs, "zip" up the front of your body to your chin, and on the out-breath drop your hands back to your thighs. Zip up again. On the third zip-up, continue your hands straight up through your face, reach high, look up, and stretch to the heavens. Be open to connecting with the radiant energies of the universe.

2. *Stretch and Bounce.* The radiant energies flow naturally, but they can become blocked by tension or stress. Simple physcial activities are often enough to revive their movement. Stand and stretch. Think of a dog or cat after a nap. Think of "making space" for your energies to flow. Stretch in all directions. Breathe deeply. Reach high and low. You can then jumpstart your energies by bouncing, jumping up and down on the balls of your feet with the rest of your body loose and relaxed. A trampoline-like bouncer is also a great aid for getting your radiant energies moving.

3. *Rub and Hug.* The soft area where the top of your neck merges into the bottom of your skull contains points that when rubbed send energies that stimulate the head, neck, and spine. Massage this area as long as and in whatever ways feel good. Then do a self-hug that stimulates and balances two of the most vital radiant circuits, called "triple warmer" and "spleen." Wrap your left hand around your

right arm with your middle finger at the indent just above your right elbow. Place your right hand under your left arm, resting on your left breast. Be still or gently rock yourself. Stay in this position for at least three deep breaths, or up to two minutes. Repeat on the other side. This can provide comfort and reduce emotional overwhelm.

4. *Dancing to the Eights.* Like the double helix of DNA, the figure-eight is one of nature's most basic patterns. Weaving your energies in figure-eight curves activates the radiant energies and brings the body into greater health and vitality. Put on music and move your hips to a figure-eight, then your arms. Flow freely, moving your entire body and creating as many small and large figure-eight patterns as feels good to you.

5. *Butt in the Air.* On its own, or after you have blown out your stress, zipped up, stretched, bounced, rubbed, hugged, and weaved your radiant energies, this exercise is a peaceful, relaxing way to further cultivate a more radiant presence. Kneel down on all fours, with your knees on the floor, push back so your butt is resting on your heels, and bring your hands to your sides as you gently lower your head to the ground. If, and only if it is comfortable to move your body and your head forward and lay your face to one side so that your butt can go higher, do so, resting like a baby. Hold this position for two or three minutes. Use the time to meditate, contemplate on a positive thought or image, list appreciations, or just let your mind go.

6. *Belt Flow.* With your fingers spread, circle your hands around the side of your body at your waist. Breathing deeply, pull from the back of your body to the front and all the way across your belly to the other side. Do this pull several times, not only at your waist, but above and below it as well. Use some pressure and a lifting movement, first using one hand, then the other, in a hand-over-hand motion. Next, on the side you are pulling toward, firmly slide both hands down the leg and off your foot. Repeat on the other side of your body. While you can do this for yourself, it is a gift you will appreciate if another person does it for you when you are lying on your back.

7. *Heaven Rushing In.* This technique is half prayer, half energy work. It connects you with the larger forces that surround you. It is particularly reviving when you are hungering for more meaning in your life or feeling despair or isolation.

   1. Step outside under the sky if possible and stand tall.
   2. Ground yourself by focusing on the sensation of your feet on the earth.

3. Inhale deeply and exhale fully.

4. Spread your fingers on your thighs.

5. With your next inhalation, slowly move your arms out to the sides and upwards, forming a circle with your hands touching, palm to palm, over your head.

6. On the exhalation, bring your hands slowly down in front of your face, coming to rest at your chest, hands in a prayer position.

7. With another deep breath, extend your arms outward to either side, lifting them slightly, and look to the heavens.

8. Sense the vastness above you and the energy around you. Receive the energies of the heavens. Allow yourself to open to a larger story. You are not alone. Feel the energies tingling through your body. Allow your arms to accumulate this energy.

9. At the center of your chest is a vortex that is traditionally known as "Heaven Rushing In." When you are ready, scoop the energies you have been accumulating in your hands into this vortex, placing the palms of both hands over the center of your chest. Allow your heart to receive this energy. You can also direct this energy to any part of your body that is tired, hurting, or that needs a boost.

You have already learned other energy techniques that stimulate the radiant circuits. The Crown Pull (p. 44) is effective. The Navel/Third-Eye Hook-Up (p. 47) is another. The latter connects two of the body's vital energy systems, known in traditional Chinese medicine as the *central vessel* and the *governing vessel*. A final technique is called the Third-Eye Tap. It is reserved for when you are already feeling good. It takes the vibration of a joyous feeling and patterns your nervous system to more easily support that vibration. The first acupuncture point on the meridian that governs the nervous system happens to be at the spot the yogis refer to as the *third eye*,

between the eyebrows, above the bridge of the nose. When you are feeling happy, deeply satisfied, spiritually connected, in love, or any other joyful feeling, you can, by tapping at your third eye, direct this energy to leave an imprint on your entire nervous system. Tap firmly yet gently. Breathe deliberately. Enjoy.

This brief overview of the radiant circuits, presented within this brief introduction to energy psychology, which is a small bandwidth within psychotherapy, offers techniques that are known to be effective; you only need use them.

Closing Words

Subtle Energy: Psychology's Missing Link

A recent mini-revolution within psychology has involved the emphatic recognition that positive thinking and "learned optimism" can be self-fulfilling. *Positive psychology*, as the trend is called (www.positivepsychology.org), can point to solid evidence showing that people who hold a positive attitude are more effective in the world, attain greater success, make more adaptive choices, stay healthier, and heal more quickly than people who are more negative in their outlook. Therapies that focus primarily on the problems and negative dimensions of a person's life may be emphasizing the wrong part of the story. A positive orientation leads to positive outcomes.

While psychology cannot lay exclusive claim to this eternal principle, it can help people to learn how to acquire attitudes that have positive repercussions in their lives. Insight, will, and intention—the commonsense approaches—are often not enough to change deep attitudes. Energy interventions, combined with methods such as visualization and affirmation, provide one of the most powerful ways of initiating such shifts. Stimulating energy points while mentally activating a problem or a goal appears to 1) create instantaneous neurological changes that, assuming the procedures are carried out properly, deactivate the biochemical underpinnings of the problem and 2) activate an energy field and related biochemical processes that promote the desired goal.

The methods can be used to promote desired psychological states as well as to counter undesired states. If a man visualizes himself attaining a well-considered goal and disturbances instantly occur in his kidney and stomach meridians, his focus and effectiveness will be compromised. If a technique is applied that remedies the energy disturbances, he can move toward the goal without conflict in the energies that influence his thought and behavior. With these obstacles removed, energy methods combined with active imagination can be introduced to surround him with an energy field that organizes his body's energy systems in a manner that corresponds with attaining the goal. Aligning the man's subtle energies with his positive intentions is a powerful intervention.

Subtle energy may long remain an elusive concept, but if you are told that a positive person carries an energy that enriches others, or a negative person carries an energy that is self-defeating, you intuitively know what is meant, even if you cannot precisely define or point to these energies. Energy psychology adds to our repertoire techniques for *identifying* the energies that are involved with psychological problems or goals and for *influencing* them to support desired outcomes. Energy interventions do not take the place of will and insight; they simply enter from a different angle and have strengths that purely psychological interventions do not have.

In that sense, energy psychology provides such a vital and missing link between intervention and outcome that psychological practices which are not attuned to the actions of subtle energy may one day be viewed as archaic. While we may never be able to adequately explain subjective experience in physical terms such as neurochemistry, or even subtle energy, an understanding of the role of subtle energy begins to fill in our understanding about many other mysteries, from the way that stimulating a set of acupuncture points can rapidly neutralize an unwanted emotional response, to the persuasively demonstrated role of focused intention on physical events, to the equally well-established telepathic exchange of information, to the many reported instances where certain personality traits of an organ donor mysteriously appear in the organ recipient, to the way positive images and prayer can facilitate healing from a distance. Psychology does not have ready explanations for such phenomena, and some formulation of an energy field that holds information—perhaps with attributes we can barely imagine, such as a macro-level version of quantum nonlocality or unfamiliar space-time relationships—is the probable missing link.

The nature of subtle energies is still shrouded in mystery, but enough is known to suggest that they influence physical health and can be harnessed to help people overcome mental problems and increase mental capacities. Subtle energies may even prove to be a link between life in a physical body and nature's archetypal or spiritual realms. A whole universe of subtle energies may, in fact, be waiting to be explored, and skillfully working with such energies is already showing great promise for empowering people to influence their own feelings, thoughts, and behavior in desired ways.

The *Energy Psychology Interactive* Self-Help Guide, with its author, primary consultants, and an advisory board composed of many of the leaders and innovators in the energy psychology field, is presented with the vivid intention that, in the face of the unprecedented challenges confronting all of us today, the program will act as a force for alleviating human suffering and elevating the human spirit. May it serve you in these ways and more.

Appendix

Taking Energy Psychology
Another Step

When you are able to precisely identify an isolated emotional response that does not serve you well (e.g., irrational fear, irrational guilt, irrational hatred, irrational jealousy) and you apply the protocol as outlined in Section I, the early clinical indications emerging from energy psychology suggest that the pattern will shift in a surprising proportion of situations. The tapping protocol is, for instance, probably a far more effective intervention than if (suppose the irrational fear were around spiders) you were simply to state an affirmation such as, "I will stay calm and relaxed whenever I see a spider." In addition to reprogramming unwanted emotional responses, reports are accumulating that the same methods can be applied with reasonable success for attaining goals. Using the tapping protocol to increase the believability when you envision an ideal response in a given situation (see p. 34) appears to translate into greater personal effectiveness with enough frequency that it is probably worth experimenting with it.

Some practitioners go so far as to recommend applying the basic protocol to all aspects of one's life. Steve Wells, a psychologist in Australia, suggests using the tapping procedure with every problem you have, and he further advises that you continue with the process until all remaining intensity about each problem is completely cleared. He recommends using the methods not only in a remedial fashion to eradicate existing problems, but also to change basic life patterns, to help create a "new future." He believes that even people who know the technique underestimate its potential for attaining greater emotional freedom and supporting their most fundamental goals and potentials.

It is too early in the field's development to know whether this optimistic assessment about the power of energy psychology is rooted mostly in an early adherent's enthusiasm or is a harbinger of a new paradigm that can endow each citizen with greater emotional freedom and control. Until research and other evidence is available, you will get the best answers from the laboratory of your own personal experimentation with the methods. Their popularity seems to be growing as increasing numbers of individuals are finding them empowering.

But what if the methods are not working for you? Assuming you are applying them precisely as they are presented and that you are not attempting to apply them in areas where the services of a qualified mental health professional are indicated (see discussion on p. 5), you would next look to physical factors and psychological factors.

Physical Factors. As indicated in Section II, when stress or fatigue interfere with the flow and balance of the energies that support brain function, energy interventions for bringing about psychological change are less effective. The most obvious first steps are to be sure you are getting enough rest and exercise and a nutritious diet. With that in place, Section II presents a set of procedures that have been found to be quite effective for optimizing the body's energies and enhancing the functioning of the nervous system to promote clear thinking, ease of learning, and overall vitality. These can be applied just prior to the tapping protocol or can be used as a daily routine or "energy vitamin" for establishing optimal energy patterns. A health professional who works directly with the body's energies can further guide you in this area.

Another factor that some practitioners feel interferes with the effectiveness of the tapping protocol in some proportion of cases involves sensitivities or subtle allergic reactions to foods (it has been estimated that over 10,000 chemical toxins have entered the food supply), medications, perfumes, specific clothing, or other environmental substances. While this is a controversial area, some people seem particularly susceptible to the effects of ingested substances and environmental conditions. These concerns are discussed further at www.allergyantidotes.com, www.naet.com, and www.alternativementalhealth.com/articles.

A third set of physical considerations involves the choice of which acupuncture points are stimulated. Many practitioners believe that for some individuals and some conditions, the protocol presented in Part I is not adequate. Different and often more elaborate protocols are applied. While a health professional capable of using more advanced methods may indeed be useful, many practitioners also believe that most people can attain at least some promising results with at least some of their issues using the basic protocol.

Psychological Factors. The most common reason that the protocol from Section I will not lead to the desired effects when properly applied is that the target problem is a component of a larger complex of emotional issues (see discussion of "aspects" on p. 30). This may indicate that work with a mental health professional is needed to overcome the problem, but often simply neutralizing the aspects of the problem is all that is necessary.

For a concrete way to understand aspects, Gary Craig, founder of EFT, uses the metaphor of a table to describe the way he approaches a problem such as generalized anxiety or incessant feelings of shame. If the presenting problem is the top of the table, the legs are the *aspects* of the problem, particularly specific events in the client's life that produced similar feelings. By chipping away at the legs, the table top often falls away spontaneously or with minimal further intervention. So rather than to begin with the "table top" or global problem, such as "I feel shame," Craig works with the "legs," addressing the problem's history—specific event by specific event—until every memory involving shame is cleared (after addressing several specific events—Craig estimates the typical range as being between 5 and 20—there is a "generalization effect" so the remainder become emotionally resolved).

Sometimes, to clear a memory, it is necessary to separate it into smaller aspects still ("the feeling of ice in my heart," "the look in her eye when she discovered me," "the sound of his voice," etc.) and treat them one at a time. Craig reports not only an extremely high success rate when focusing on these micro-aspects of a problem, but also that the gains are far more durable than when only using a global (table top) formulation of the problem. Craig's website, www.emofree.com, has a powerful search engine where you can find discussions of EFT with hundreds of specific issues.

When Professional Help Is Needed. The psychotherapy community has become increasingly sophisticated and able in addressing a wide range of emotional problems. If you have taken this program as far as you can and the problems of concern persist, seriously consider seeking outside help. Or if after simply bringing focus to an issue you find yourself emotionally overwhelmed, this may indicate that a problem has been brewing and is begging for your attention. Effective resources are available. Finding the *right* therapist is an important choice. Both competence and compatibility are critical factors. Talk with friends and local professionals about possible referrals. Any of many websites may also be of value in helping you find the right therapist, such as www.psych.org/public_info/PDF/psythera.pdf, http://helping.apa.org/find.html, www.therapistlocator.net, and www.find-a-therapist.com. Also, see Links and Resources (p. 81) for lists of therapists who utilize an energy perspective.

Basic Tapping Sequence

Preliminaries: Three Thumps/Three Navel Touch, Select Problem, Rate Problem from 1 to 10, Word the "Reminder Phrase."

Part 1: Rub chest sore spot while saying three times, "Even though [name problem], I deeply love and accept myself."

Part 2: Tap the points (see below) while saying out loud your reminder phrase.

Part 3: Tap the point between the little and fourth finger, beneath the knuckle as you: look down to the right, down to the left, circle eyes, circle in opposite direction, hum a bar of a song, count to five, hum again, sweep your eyes out and up.

Part 4: Repeat Part 2.

Part 5: Rate problem again. If above 0, return to Part 1 and repeat sequence. If at 0 or near 0, imagine having an ideal response in the situation, rate it on how plausible this seems (0 to 10), and repeat Parts 1–4, this time using a reminder phrase that represents your ideal response and visualizing your ideal response as you tap. Repeat sequence until believability is up to 8 or higher. Then you are ready to test the gains in a "real-life" setting.

The tapping points (see illustration on p. 22):

> Inside of eyebrows
> Outside of eyes
> Under eyes
> Under nose
> Under lower lip
> K-27 points
> Over thymus
> Spleen points (4 inches below underarms)
> Side of legs between hip and knee
> Karate chop points
> Point between the little and fourth finger, beneath the knuckle

How Does Energy Psychology Work?

You are probably aware that chemical imbalances are involved in psychological problems such as anxiety and depression. Evidence is mounting that the body's energies are also involved in emotional disturbances, and that interventions into the body's energy system can shift the brain chemistry in a way that helps overcome many psychological problems. The interventions you have been learning have been effective in a wide range of situations, including helping people during major disasters and the aftermath of trauma. They make use of a simple process you already know: comforting yourself using your own hands and your own words.

Your hands carry an electromagnetic charge, and your body's energies include the electrical charge in every cell and organ, the electrical pathways in the nervous system, the electromagnetic fields surrounding every organ as well as the entire body, and also more subtle energies, such as the *chi* spoken of by acupuncturists and the *prana* spoken of by yoga practitioners. With psychological problems, an experience you regularly encounter causes your brain to send out electrical signals that lead to an emotion (perhaps anxiety, depression, or anger), a perception, or a behavior that is not appropriate for the current situation. The triggering experience may be one you encounter with some frequency, such as being in situations where you feel tested, but it also may be internal, a recurring memory, image, or thought. One way to approach the problem is to work directly with the energies that maintain the pattern in your brain's response to the triggering experience. That is the approach used in energy psychology.

For instance, if every time you think about a particular situation, certain parts of your brain become overstimulated, leading to emotions that get in your way, you can think about the situation while you touch or tap or massage trigger points that alter the dysfunctional response in your brain. This retrains your body and brain so that the thought or situation no longer causes the over-reaction. The trigger points are often the same points that are used in acupuncture, though needles are not necessary to achieve the desired effect. This process alone can overcome many emotional and psychological problems.

If we try to understand the claimed speed and effectiveness of acupoint stimulation with problems such as anxiety in terms of insight, cognitive restructuring, reward and punishment, or even the curative powers of the therapeutic relationship, the treatment outcomes make no sense. If we examine electrochemical shifts in brain chemistry that are brought about by stimulating acupuncture points, however, a coherent hypothesis begins to emerge. The electrochemical basis of the reported clinical outcomes of stimulating acupuncture points in the treatment of anxiety can be summarized as follows:

> Stimulating acupuncture points while simultaneously activating an anxiety-provoking image changes the neurological connections to the amygdala and other brain structures in a manner that reduces the anxious response to that image.

This summary of the actions of stimulating acupuncture points is based on three empirically demonstrated principles:

1. Brain wave patterns that are markers of anxiety have been identified and are generally accepted.

2. Stimulating a given acupuncture point sends signals to given parts of the brain. A study by Hui and others, coming out of Harvard Medical School in 2000, concludes: "These preliminary results [based upon functional MRI readings] suggest that acupuncture needle manipulation modulates the activity of the limbic system and subcortical structures. We hypothesize that modulation of subcortical structures may be an important mechanism by which acupuncture exerts its complex multi-system effects."

3. A research program conducted by Joseph LeDoux at NYU shows that reactivating a memory makes it vulnerable to events that can change the connections to and from the amygdala that are implicated in conditioned fear.

Brain wave studies conducted by Joaquín Andrade, M.D. (a member of the *EPI* Advisory Board), demonstrate how these principles converge so that stimulating certain acupuncture points while an anxiety-evoking image has been activated sends signals that normalize the affected wave patterns (see brain scan images on the CD that is part of the *EPI* program for professionals).

Neutralizing an anxiety-evoking thought, image, or memory in this manner is rapid and tends to be permanent. This is one of the core procedures being advanced within energy psychology. Acupuncture points, charted thousands of years ago, have low electrical resistance as well as high concentrations of receptors that are responsive to mechanical stimulation of the skin. Tapping, massaging, or holding them, as well as more invasive procedures like the use of needles or electrical impulses, activates signals that go to various brain centers and appear potent in shifting brain wave patterns, often bringing disturbed patterns, as seen on brain scans, to within normal range.

Preliminary Report of the First Large-Scale Study of Energy Psychology

In preliminary clinical trials involving more than 31,400 patients from 11 allied treatment centers in South America during a 14-year period, a variety of randomized, controlled pilot studies were conducted. In one of these, approximately 5,000 patients diagnosed at intake with an anxiety disorder were randomly assigned to an experimental group (stimulation of selected acupuncture points) or a control group (Cognitive Behavior Therapy/medication). Ratings were given by independent clinicians who interviewed each patient at the close of therapy, at 1 month, at 3 months, at 6 months, and at 12 months. The raters made a determination of complete remission of symptoms, partial remission of symptoms, or no clinical response. The raters did not know if the patient received CBT/medication or energy interventions. They knew only the initial diagnosis, the symptoms, and the severity, as judged by the intake staff. At the close of therapy:

63% of the control group were judged as having improved.
90% of the experimental group were judged as having improved.

51% of the control group were judged as being symptom free.
76% of the experimental group were judged as being symptom free.

At one-year follow-up, the patients receiving acupoint treatments were substantially less prone to relapse or partial relapse than those receiving CBT/medication, as indicated by the independent raters' assessments and corroborated by brain imaging and neurotransmitter profiles. In a related pilot study by the same team, the length of treatment was substantially shorter with energy interventions and associated methods than with CBT/medication (mean = 3 sessions vs. mean = 15 sessions).

If subsequent research corroborates these early findings, it will be a notable development since CBT/medication is currently the established standard of care for anxiety disorders and the greater effectiveness of the energy approach suggested by this study would be highly significant. The preliminary nature of these findings must, however, be emphasized. The study was initially envisioned as an in-house assessment of a new method and was not designed with publication in mind. Not all of the variables that need to be controlled in robust research were tracked, not all criteria were defined with rigorous precision, the record-keeping was relatively informal, and source data were not always maintained. Nonetheless, the studies all used randomized samples, control groups, and blind assessment. The findings were so striking that the team decided to report them. A full report can be found on the *Energy Psychology Interactive* CD. The principal investigator was Joaquín Andrade, M.D.

The Body's Energies

The human brain has some 100 billion neurons that each connect electrochemically with up to 10,000 other neurons. If you focus on the brain's electrical impulses instead of its physical matter, it is an incomprehensibly complex energy system, but it is also a natural focus for psychology. Modern brain-imaging technology is being applied to increase our understanding of almost any psychological process being seriously studied. Meanwhile, using non-intrusive and readily accessible methods for understanding and affecting the body's electrical and other energies, energy psychology provides a direct approach for working with the body's energy system.

Few concepts in the healing arts have been used more loosely than *energy*. While energy takes many forms, it is commonly defined as *a force that produces a physical change* ("the capacity of a physical system to do work"). Locomotives were propelled with the *thermal* energy released by burning coal. A bowling ball scatters the pins with the *kinetic* energy it delivers by virtue of its motion. *Chemical* energy, released as different substances react to one another, can be harnessed in the batteries that play a walkman or start a car. *Nuclear* energy, until it is released to power a submarine or devastate a city, holds together the nucleus of an atom. Whereas nuclear energy originates in the core of an atom, *electrical* current involves the flow of electrons that normally orbit that core.

Wherever there is an electrical current, it creates and is surrounded by an electromagnetic field. Each cell of the body functions like a miniature battery, with chemical reactions producing electrical current and an electromagnetic field. The negative polarity is outside the cell membrane; the positive polarity is inside. The human body is composed of 75 trillion such "batteries." From the cells to the organs to the entire body, we are electromagnetic fields within fields within fields. Instruments for identifying and measuring our electrical and electromagnetic energies, from the voltameter to the MRI, have long existed and are ever being refined.

Subtle Energies

The physical world appears through the eye of nuclear physics to be a latticework of energies; the atomic building blocks of matter vibrate dynamically and resemble waves as much as particles. The body's complex network of electrical and electromagnetic energies seems to intersect with an even more complex network of subtle energy systems that permeate the body. Subtle energy is energy that we do not know how to detect directly but which, like gravity, we know by its effects. Most basic is the "life force." When it is there, you are alive; when it is not there, even if your cells are still alive, you are dead. While an intuitively easy notion, neither the life force nor other forms of subtle energy have been registered by even our most sensitive physical instruments.

In fact, while kinetic, thermal, chemical, electrical, and nuclear energies have been well mapped, the subtle energies that are of concern to energy psychology remain outside the Western scientific paradigm. These energies have, however, been recognized by many societies throughout history, and detailed expositions about specific kinds of subtle energy found in the literature of numerous cultures are beginning to stand up to scientific scrutiny (see William Collinge's *Subtle Energy*, 1998; Richard Gerber's *Vibrational Medicine*, 2001; and James Oschman's *Energy Medicine*, 2000).

The meridian pathways that are said to carry the *chi* energy that governs both the material and the "subtle body," for instance (but not *chi* itself), are being verified using physical instrumentation. Mapped some 5,000 years ago by Chinese physicians, the meridians did not correspond with any known anatomical structures and were easily dismissed by Western scientists. But in 1985, French scientists injected radioactive technetium into several of the traditional acupuncture points of their subjects and traced the isotope's uptake using gamma-camera imaging. The technetium migrated along the classical meridian pathways for a distance of thirty centimeters in four to six minutes. Technetium injected into non-acupuncture points tended to simply pool. This study in part replicated findings reported in Korea in the 1960s, and various other studies have identified physiological correlates of the meridian system (See Gerber's *Vibrational Medicine*, pp. 122–127).

Organizations such as the International Society for the Study of Subtle Energy and Energy Medicine (www.issseem.org) are producing newsletters and professional journals that scientifically investigate subtle energy.

Thought and Subtle Energy

Thought, according to recent compelling evidence, influences and is influenced by subtle energy, difficult to measure but wielding a discernible impact on the physical world. At least 200 published studies demonstrate physical effects of visualization and prayer on people, animals, plants, organs, blood, and cells. For instance, a person can change the Galvanic skin response of another person at another location by directing calming thoughts, or angry thoughts, toward that person. Cardiac patients who were prayed for had a lower chance of cardiac arrest during stressful procedures than those in a control group. Most people can be taught within a single session how to use visualization and focused intention to markedly influence the rate that blood cells in a test tube in another room will deteriorate (each of these studies, and hundreds of others, are summarized in Daniel Benor's *Spiritual Healing: Scientific Validation of a Healing Revolution*, 2001).

Energy psychology is based in part on evidence that thought affects the meridians and other energies, and also that disturbances in these energies lead to disturbances in thought and other psychological processes. This two-way effect is the domain of energy psychology. The field's promise is in its claims to have developed a set of readily accessible procedures for assessing and shifting the energies that are believed to maintain dysfunctional habits of thought, emotion, and behavior.

Principles of Energy Medicine

Energy psychology is the branch of **energy medicine** that applies an understanding of the body's energies to psychological issues. *Energy medicine* recognizes energy as a vital, living, moving force that determines much about health and happiness. In energy medicine, energy is the *medicine*, and energy is also the *patient*. You heal the body by activating its natural healing energies; you also heal the body by restoring energies that have become weak, disturbed, or out of balance. Energy medicine is both a complement to other approaches to medical care and a complete system for self-care and self-help. It can address physical illness and emotional or mental disorders, and can also promote high-level wellness and peak performance. The essential principles of energy medicine include (based on Donna Eden's *Energy Medicine*):

1. Energies—both electromagnetic energies and more subtle energies— form the dynamic *infrastructure* of the physical body.

2. The health of those energies–in terms of flow, balance, and harmony–is reflected in the health of the body.

3. Conversely, when the body is not healthy, corresponding disturbances in its energies can be identified and treated.

4. To overcome illness and maintain vibrant health, the body needs its energies to:

   a. *Move* and have space to continue to move—energies may become blocked due to toxins, muscular or other constriction, prolonged stress, or interference from other energies.

   b. *Move in specific patterns*—generally in harmony with the physical structures and functions that the energies animate and support. "Flow follows function."

   c. *Cross over*—at all levels, from the microlevel of the double helix of DNA, extending to the macrolevel where the left side of the brain controls the right side of the body and the right side to the left.

   d. *Maintain a balance* with other energies—the energies may lose their natural balance due to prolonged stress or other conditions that keep specific energy systems in a survival mode.

5. Flow, balance, and harmony can be non-invasively restored and maintained within an energy system by:

   a. *tapping, massaging, pinching, twisting,* or *connecting* specific energy points on the skin

   b. *tracing* or *swirling* the hand over the skin along specific energy pathways

   c. *exercises* or *postures* designed for specific energetic effects

   d. focused *use of the mind* to move specific energies

   e. *surrounding an area* with healing energies (one person's energies impacts another's)

Links and Resources

Video Programs Similar to the Approach in this Handbook:
www.eft-innovations.com/video_main.htm (2-video-tape set by
  Patricia Carrington, Ph.D.)
www.emofree.com/store/ordervcd.asp (Gary Craig's introduction to
  EFT)
www.emofree.com/products.htm (Gary Craig's complete foundational
  video program)

Free Internet Support e-mail Lists and Support Sites (for support regarding energy psychology and psychotherapy, consider):
www.emofree.com/email.htm (Emotional Freedom Techniques e-mail
  support list)
www.eftsupport.com (Emotional Freedom Techniques support site)
www.unstressforsuccess.com (Tapas Acupressure technique support
  site)

http://groups.yahoo.com/group/Meridian-Energy (Meridian Therapy Discussion Group)

Free Newsletters/Reports (Go to the website listed to subscribe):

www.eft-innovations.com (*Emotional Freedom Techniques Innovations*)

www.energypsychresearch.org/ (Reports Research Findings in Energy Psychology)

www.wholistichealingresearch.com (Wholistic Healing Research Newsletter)

www.ijhc.org (*International Journal of Healing and Caring*)

Practitioner Referral Lists:

www.energypsych.com (Energy Diagnostic and Treatment Methods)

www.emofree.com/Practitioners/referralMain.asp (Emotional Freedom Techniques)

www.eftsupport.com/practstatelist.htm (Emotional Freedom Techniques)

www.matrixwork.org/directory.htm (Seemorg Matrix Work)

Nonprofit Organizations Concerned with Energy Psychology:

www.energypsych.org (Association for Comprehensive Energy Psychology, ACEP)

www.theamt.com (Association for Meridian Therapies)

www.energymed.org (Energy Medicine Institute)

www.issseem.org (International Society for the Study of Subtle Energies and Energy Medicine, ISSSEEM)

To learn more about the full *Energy Psychology Interactive* program for health care professionals, visit www.EnergyPsychologyInteractive.com.

Notes

PROGRAMS FOR RESTORING AND REVITALIZING THE HUMAN ENERGY SYSTEM
by
Donna Eden
and
David Feinstein, Ph.D.

Energy Medicine
Energy Psychology
Energies of Love

INNERSOURCE
Empowering Body, Mind, and Spirit

Books

Videos

CDs/DVDs

Seminars

Free e-Groups

Home Study CE

www.innersource.net

24-hour Order Line
Request Product List:
1-800-835-8332

To learn more about the full *Energy Psychology Interactive* program for health care professionals, visit www.EnergyPsychologyInteractive.com.